Effective Technical Leadership

An Introduction for Engineering Executives

Koso Brown

Copyright 2024© Koso Brown

All rights reserved. This book is copyrighted and no part of it may be reproduced, distributed, or transmitted in any form or by any means, including photocopying, recording, or other electronic or mechanical methods, without the prior written permission of the publisher, except in the case of brief quotations embodied in critical reviews and certain other non-commercial uses permitted by copyright law.

Printed in the United States of America

Copyright 2024© Koso Brown

Contents

Introduction 1

Chapter 1 2

Technical leadership: what is it?................................ 2

Chapter 2 13

The Importance of Technical Proficiency in Leadership
.... 13

Chapter 3 17

Crucial Attributes of an Excellent Technical Leader ... 17

Chapter 4 25

Use Flow to track your development as a technical leader. 25

Chapter 5 33

Myths and Misconceptions about Technical Leadership
.... 33

Final Thought 41

Introduction

The majority of prosperous projects have a single engineer in charge of advancing the project and making sure that confident, sound technical judgments are made. That individual is usually called a Tech Lead. Rather than managing staff, they frequently mentor them to produce their best work.

Technically proficient leaders are essential for DeVos and engineers creating intricate goods. Although they can design a plan, engineering managers don't necessarily have the know-how to carry it out. Fortunately, technical leadership allows you to strike a balance between technical expertise and management. Technical leadership, to put it simply, is a set of abilities and knowledge that blends technical know-how with management. Similar to this, a tech lead—also referred to as a technical leader—is a specialized position that uses this understanding. We'll go over the ins and outs of technical leadership, whether you want to become one yourself or just know how to recognize a good one.

Chapter 1

Technical leadership: what is it?

The capacity to oversee and assist a group of engineers and developers is known as technical leadership. It specifically calls for a leader who is aware of the limitations and possibilities of the technology they are developing or utilizing. The foundation of excellent technical leadership is your capacity to make important choices and your faith in your team to carry out the technical aspects of the project.

For engineers who want to expand their technical and management skill sets, tech leaders are a typical position. Tech leads collaborate with their teams to achieve project goals after product owners and stakeholders have shaped them. Tech leads could concentrate on a certain area of production they are knowledgeable about along the process.

Technical leads oversee a project from inception to completion; they manage their team, suggest technical fixes, and communicate with other departments. In summary, technical leaders ensure that a project's technical and human components work together.

Adaptive versus technical leadership

Technical and adaptive leadership provide various problems that require special answers. Adaptive leadership uses innovation and experimentation to address unconventional issues. Technical leadership frequently makes use of adaptive pivots along with more conventional ideas. Technical leadership can therefore seem like a combination of soft skills and development.

Technical leadership: Definition and characteristics of effective leaders

Managers manage several teams and assign tasks, while tech leads provide technical knowledge and direction to certain teams and projects. These positions provide teams with essential guidance and support. Tech leads, on the other hand, handle high-level duties while advocating for engineers or personally solving problems.

What is the job of a tech lead?

Technical leaders manage and do technical activities simultaneously. They not only manage team members but also provide hands-on assistance with workflow procedures. The duties of a technical leader consist of:

- ❖ **Guiding leadership:** Within an organization, technical leaders answer to supervisors and other managers. They can inform high-level planning and report on the success or failure of a project.

- ❖ **Training the team members:** Under a technical leader, teams pick up new abilities and learn how to use their tech stack. Tech leads should support the development of every team member. They can help with employment decisions as well.

- ❖ **Putting solutions into practice:** Technical leaders support their teams in developing solutions so they may close gaps or advance the creation of new products. They also mentor their colleagues through problems and obstacles related to technology.

- ❖ **Giving system expertise:** Tech leads oversee changes to the system and make sure all software is updated. To avoid security threats, they could additionally audit these systems' security.
- ❖ **Assigning duties:** Technical leaders are aware of the advantages and disadvantages of each team member. They assign roles appropriately when they take on a project.
- ❖ **promoting project success:** Outstanding technical leaders set realistic expectations and, where feasible, go above and above. They identify effective solutions to issues by monitoring KPIs, examining user requirements, and using past performance.
- ❖ **Leading a team:** Like managers, tech leads provide direction and support to teams. Tech leaders facilitate cooperation, manage daily standups, support teams, and share

resources.

Technical abilities for leadership

We'll go over the fundamentals of technical leadership to assist you in acquiring the hard and soft skills required in each area.

Soft skills

Not every exceptional technical leader has practical experience. Your success may be determined by the qualities and attitudes you bring to the table. Technical leadership is enhanced by soft skills and characteristics such as:

- ❖ **Action/solution-oriented:** proactively seeking answers to problems as they emerge
- ❖ **Transparent communication:** proactive, regular dialogue with groups
- ❖ **Organization:** Setting priorities when handling several activities at once

- ❖ **Empathy:** the capacity to take into account the opinions and feelings of team members
- ❖ **Adaptability:** a readiness to examine alternative viewpoints
- ❖ **Creative thinking:** identifying unconventional answers to issues
- ❖ **Resilience:** the capacity to guide groups through difficult development cycles

Technical skills

Technical leadership is distinguished from other styles of management by technical expertise. It needs:

- ❖ **Tooling and prototyping:** the capacity to quickly prototype concepts or solutions and familiarity with instruments that expedite this procedure
- ❖ **Constant delivery and improvement:** knowledge of CI/CD techniques and tools for automating the development, testing, and deployment of apps
- ❖ **Progress:** taking part in engineering, development, and coding
- ❖ **Evaluations:** Evaluate teams' work when

required to make sure it complies with technical requirements for your organization or when a technical issue needs to be resolved but is either extremely complicated or falls within your area of expertise.

- ❖ **Management of resources:** making certain teams can stay within budget and on schedule
- ❖ **Maintenance of the system:** using and preserving cloud, database, security, and version control systems
- ❖ **Optimizing performance:** Maintaining your infrastructure, domain expertise, and industry trends up to date helps enhance team performance

Leadership skills

Technical leadership requires managerial experience. In particular, you need to be able to manage:

- ❖ **Providing and getting input:** providing sympathetic comments on the work of teams and taking criticism in kind
- ❖ **Encouraging dialogue:** considering feedback from stakeholders and the team to promote communication
- ❖ **Reaction to crisis:** addressing a problem, obstacle, or communication breakdown in a composed and efficient manner
- ❖ **Management of a team:** settling disputes and promoting collaboration through inclusive leadership

- ❖ **The quality of operations:** The team's performance is under the technical leader's control. This could involve controlling cycle time and pull request size or gauging the time and resources spent on particular projects.

- ❖ **Coding:** Finding a balance between their coding and non-coding obligations is a challenge faced by many tech leaders. They either quit coding altogether or continue to code full-time. You mustn't disregard technical tasks as a technical leader.

- ❖ **Code Evaluations:** While it's not advisable to evaluate every change made to the codebase, a technical leader may wish to train inexperienced developers or recent hires by conducting code reviews. You need to adopt a coaching stance and make sure that everything is understood, including the benefits of a certain strategy and the rationale behind your actions.

- ❖ **Solving problems:** recognizing and fixing problems that teams face

Management Skills

Management-related abilities are additional essential competencies for a tech leader. A few developers are not interested in learning about managerial duties. Others will inevitably start exhibiting the following abilities required for advancement to the position of technical leader.

- ❖ **Problem-solving:** Technical leaders must actively participate in putting solutions into practice rather than only recognizing issues.

- ❖ **Possess a likable personality:** One of a leader's main duties is to establish deep connections. To accomplish team and organizational goals, IT leaders and team managers need to build trust with company executives as well as the team members they'll be collaborating with regularly.

- ❖ **Project management:** A leader is in charge of organizing and carrying out tasks as well as scheduling the time of their group. Technical leaders frequently view their work from a high-level, long-term perspective.

❖ **Crisis management:** There are good days and bad days for every leader. Even in the most trying circumstances, the more effective leaders seem to always be in control, remain composed under pressure, and can steady the ship.

Chapter 2

The Importance of Technical Proficiency in Leadership

The subject of whether or not leadership is a technical skill may confound most individuals! It is primarily a differentiable skill from technical abilities such as data analysis or coding. However, it has to do with having the ability to successfully lead, mentor, and inspire people. Few concepts and tactics are related to leadership; instead, it is more strongly associated with soft and interpersonal abilities than with technical ones.

Turn Technical Knowledge into Leadership

Technical leadership is a complex role that includes essential management, leadership duties, and in-depth technical knowledge. It primarily has to do with decision-making, strategic planning, and efficient communication. Both great technical proficiency and strategic acumen are essential for a technical leader. Leading teams, making sure they are in line with company objectives, motivating team members, keeping lines of communication open, and fostering a cooperative work atmosphere are the first duties of the position.

Technical prowess can be demonstrated by a leader via their ability to work and solve problems. A team is more likely to respect and follow the leader when they witness commitment and the capacity to handle challenging technical problems. For instance, a software developer with experience can use their knowledge of coding to inspire a group of people to create creative software solutions. Effective communication is another aspect of leadership, and a skilled leader can communicate technical concepts in a way that team members can grasp. Effective communication also helps close the gap between a team and a leader. A data scientist, for instance, can provide a marketing team with an explanation of complicated algorithms that they can utilize to make decisions.

Integration leadership and technical roles:

Technical leaders frequently have to strike a balance between their new leadership responsibilities and their technical obligations. They have to balance both areas at the same time, which makes this act difficult.

Good Communication

Effective communication is essential to leadership, yet motivating people and expressing ideas clearly and concisely can be difficult. It can be difficult to build effective communication skills, especially when working with big or varied teams.

Team Dynamics

It can be difficult to comprehend and manage different personalities and points of view while working with varied teams, which is a requirement of leadership. It can be difficult for leaders to maintain a professional relationship with their staff while also setting personal limits. To cultivate their leadership abilities, leaders must modify their approach to better fit the needs of their team.

Getting Used to Change

Technical leaders have to adjust to new procedures, instruments, or techniques because technology is constantly evolving, and this can be quite difficult at times. They can find it difficult to improve if they don't accept the adjustments.

Strategic vision

Technical leaders frequently have to take on immediate technical issues to generate distinctive strategic thinking for the team.

Chapter 3

Crucial Attributes of an Excellent Technical Leader

It is impossible to exaggerate the value of teamwork, communication, and fostering strong bonds in technical leadership. Technically proficient leaders who are strong in these domains foster creativity, assemble competent teams, and overcome obstacles. Technical leaders can successfully negotiate the complexities of their roles and propel company success by adopting these qualities.

Creating Powerful Bonds

Developing great relationships with teammates and coworkers is essential as it helps foster a positive work atmosphere, boost morale, and increase trust. The foundation of a leader's influence is these relationships.

As an illustration, An IT leader can foster a positive

working atmosphere, forge strong bonds with IT support personnel, and guarantee that support personnel are driven to provide top-notch service.

Techniques: Effective leaders take the time to get to know their team members, empathetically communicate, offer assistance, and have candid conversations about professional growth.

Communication

Since good technical leadership requires excellent communication, leaders must make the transition from technical to everyday language so that team members can understand their directives and goals.

As an illustration, to put it simply, a team leader in charge of software development simplifies difficult coding ideas so that the marketing division may better collaborate.

Techniques: To improve their abilities, leaders might employ a few different tactics by simplifying difficult technical ideas with the use of metaphors, analogies, and visual aids. To create a clean environment, promote regular feedback, open communication, and active listening.

Collaborating

Utilizing the varied talents of technical teams requires collaboration skills. Productivity increases, creativity, and better problem-solving are all results of effective teamwork. Navigating different ideas, work styles, and personalities within a team may be challenging, though.

As an illustration Cross-functional cooperation between software developers and quality assurance testers can be facilitated by a project manager, which speeds up problem-solving and produces better results.

Techniques: By encouraging teamwork, establishing clear goals, and appreciating team members' contributions, a leader can cultivate a collaborative culture.

How to develop into a technical leader

You can prepare yourself for the role of tech lead, even though it might seem challenging at first. We'll discuss the most common path to becoming a technical leader, however, there are other options as well. If you choose to alter, add, or delete any of these steps, you can still succeed as a tech lead.

Build up your team

You require a team once you've been offered a technical leadership position. Select a group of reliable specialists that you get along with, whether it's for a single project or multiple ones. Some of these team members will be introduced to you as you advance through the levels. Always remember that selecting engineers you personally like should come second to the team's overall cohesion.

You might also have the opportunity to expand your

team by hiring additional members. When you hire outside workers, you will work with principle learning engineers to coach and train them in your processes. You'll be more successful if you can impart more experience and if your team gains more knowledge.

Look for a job

Applying for tech lead positions is possible once you have the necessary expertise. Internships and training courses can sometimes help you advance quickly into the position. In other situations, you must find the role on your own. Remember the following advice while looking for tech lead positions:

- ✓ On your résumé, list all of your engineering and managerial experience.

- ✓ Emphasize your areas of expertise in your cover letter.
- ✓ Ask your trainers and other tech leads about their hiring procedures to help you prepare

for the interview process.

- ✓ When feasible, provide examples of your previous work and code.

Participate in technical leadership development

It takes time and training to combine technical and managerial talents, so you should always be attending training sessions to stay up to date on the processes and assignments that lie ahead of you. Project management and technical skill training is available both in-person and online through colleges and commercial businesses. Even if you might already possess some of the necessary abilities, it's always a good idea to be safe.

Understand the duties of a technical leader.

You should consider your options at this stage of the process. You could work as a senior team member instead of taking on leadership based on your technical skills. Alternatively, you might consider going into management. Before taking on the role of technical leader, make sure that this is the best course for you.

To comprehend what a technical leader is expected to do, discover:

- ✓ The various methods of testing and reviewing that you use
- ✓ How to operate the software needed for the position
- ✓ The requirements for quality assurance that you must fulfill
- ✓ Regulations about the work you would oversee
- ✓ IT guidelines for businesses operating in your industry

Obtain managerial expertise.

Seek opportunities to develop managerial skills after demonstrating your proficiency in a certain area. Remember that you can obtain this experience without holding a manager position. You can get management experience by taking on side projects, coaching up-and-coming developers, and monitoring performance. Along with introducing you to new technical abilities, this process will provide you with leadership models to think about.

Learn something in the technical sector.

Aspiring tech leaders should first understand their industry, usually through college or work experience, before considering management. Degrees in computer science and engineering can teach the abilities and information required for the position. Programs for degrees also enable you to compare several fields before making a choice.

However, excellent technical leaders can also pick up knowledge through practical experience. Jobs in programming and web development can all be excellent starting points. This practical method also provides you with an insider's viewpoint on the industry.

The objective is to acquire the knowledge and

expertise required for technical leadership, regardless of the route you select. With this technical understanding, seek out chances to demonstrate your leadership abilities. As you transition into leadership, you can lead minor projects, mentor more junior staff members, and develop your technical expertise.

Chapter 4

Use Flow to track your development as a technical leader.

Technical leadership is based on teamwork and leadership abilities. Whether you want to become a tech lead or just want to get better at technical leadership, by following these guidelines you can help your teams innovate, produce amazing products, and develop. Technical leaders who monitor the performance of their teams require a platform such as Flow. Performance data is arranged on an easy-to-read dashboard by Flow. It also provides the strategic insights required to lessen ineffective work and conflict within the team.

Principal Characteristic Technical Leadership Qualities

Two components of your skill set are technical and managerial. But personality attributes are just one aspect of what makes a leader; there are many more. The ensuing segment delineates some fundamental characteristics of technical leadership. These are viewpoints and a manner of thinking, not just characteristics.

Open to New Ideas

Trying out novel concepts fosters a sense of camaraderie. Technical leadership entails experimenting with novel concepts while taking possible hazards into account. A tech lead shouldn't be scared to take calculated risks. Any technical leader should possess critical thinking skills since it is an essential component of making decisions of this nature. Moreover, a leader who practices critical thinking can spot possible issues and keep an engineering team's technologies, goods, and procedures evolving.

Communication

Communication is essential; in fact, it frequently causes friction in teams. especially in the present, when remote work environments and asynchronous communication are so important to development teams.

Expressing what a solution should look like and recognizing whether or not all team members share the same vision of the solution are key components of clear communication. Invite developers to contribute and listen to their thoughts if they have a different approach.

While taking logical steps to solve the issue at hand, resolve any disputes that may arise within the team, and show empathy. Your logical decisions should be in line with your comprehensive vision for the company and the development of your team members.

Know Your Team

You need to approach a business challenge from several angles to solve it as best you can. Every team member has a different set of abilities as well as strengths and shortcomings. The technical leader must assess the team's strengths and shortcomings and devise a plan for allocating responsibilities that will foster the group's development. In addition, a leader needs to establish a rapport with the team members to guide and motivate them to go beyond their comfort zones.

Organized and Implemented Measures

One ability that any leader needs to have is the ability to take decisive action. But it's crucial to understand how to arrange and divide a business requirement into more manageable, digestible parts. Tech leads are required to map the many components and their connections to the various team members, as well as design the architectural framework of the business challenge.

Wide-ranging and Holistic Viewpoint

To address an issue, a technical leader looks beyond their technical knowledge alone. Rather, you take into account various team members', consumers', and the organization's perspectives. You think about how your choices will impact each team member as well as the organization's overall growth. You consider the long-term implications of a choice rather than just yourself and your group.

Pay attention to mental health

Individuals still feel uncomfortable talking about their mental health issues. Being a leader is having empathy and letting the team know that we're all weak and in need of support. Are you aware that a lot of nations have policies and procedures in place to give employees' mental health a top priority? Having a required annual vacation is one such measure. Employees are encouraged to take time off from their work and concentrate on themselves by offering vacations. It aids in their return to productivity and concentration.

Employees at many companies are now able to work remotely since remote work is growing in popularity. The biggest benefit of working remotely is that you may cut costs on infrastructure and office space. Additionally, workers could enhance their work-life balance by planning their workload more effectively and saving hours on their commute.

Thus, find out what the employee would prefer to work and give them that flexibility. Plan "Team Bonding" or "Team Integration" events for at least a quarter if your team isn't meeting often to promote open communication and a positive team environment. You may create a safe space for your team to communicate in this way. In general, a leader needs to be an excellent listener. You should "Listen to Understand" rather than merely "Listen to Reply."

Eliminate the bad stuff.

You read correctly. It's never about tagging on extras. A holistic approach requires the elimination of some harmful behaviors.

- ❖ **Bias:** You cannot make impartial conclusions if you are biased.
- ❖ **Extended working hours:** You won't be able to give the work your all if you work over your designated working hours. Your staff will become frustrated and worn out if you, as the leader, expect them to labor for hours on end.
- ❖ **unpleasant workplace:** In the end, all these negative aspects will have a detrimental effect and result in an unpleasant workplace.
- ❖ **Working in silos:** The team won't be able to accomplish its goals if its members operate independently and don't cooperate. The majority of time and effort are wasted.
- ❖ **Lack of transparency:** Members of the team cannot work together productively if there is a lack of transparency. Transparent communication is beneficial.

❖ **Lack of appreciation and inspiration:** Your team members won't be inspired to put in more effort and their best efforts if you don't recognize their contributions.

Chapter 5

Myths and Misconceptions about Technical Leadership

Let's start by dispelling some common myths and misconceptions about technical leadership.

- ❖ **You need a leadership title to be a technical leader.** Finally, you don't need a particular title or position on the team to be a technical leader. Long before you hold the appropriate title, you will need to adopt the habits and use your leadership abilities if you want to advance in your profession.

- ❖ **You have to decide on all technical matters as a technical leader.** This is untrue. Even if your vote might break ties, you still must give other engineers a chance to decide. If you were in charge of every choice, you would impede your team's progress and end up acting as a bottleneck.

- ❖ **You should tackle all the trickiest difficulties since you are the most skilled**

engineer. Once more, this is untrue. Even though you might take on some of the most challenging issues, giving others advice and putting them in a position to succeed in solving those challenging issues can lead to greater progress for you and the team.

As you advance to become a potent technical leader

You may be anxious about what will happen next if you are given the chance to lead a team. You can see yourself having a nervous and unclear day. You may start reaping the rewards after your plan and goal are established. Being an effective technical leader benefits you personally as well as the success of your group and company.

Creating a Technical Strategy and Vision

You can create a technical vision and plan for your project as you grow as a technical leader. It will assist you in creating a project plan that is both strategic and transparent. The following advice will help you create a technological vision and plan:

- ✓ Engage stakeholders to guarantee that all parties are in agreement.
- ✓ Make use of flexibility and agility to make sure the plan can quickly adjust to changes.
- ✓ Provide insightful metrics to monitor development and promptly determine success and failure.
- ✓ Pay attention to ongoing technological innovation and progress
- ✓ Establish a collaborative and accountable culture
- ✓ Allow for flexibility and scalability to satisfy ever-changing client needs
- ✓ Make judgments and assign assignments based on information or figures.
- ✓ Establish a collaborative and accountable culture
- ✓ Pay attention to ongoing technological innovation and progress

- ✓ Provide insightful metrics to monitor

development and promptly determine success and failure

Promote Originality

As a good technical leader, you can assist teams in coming up with fresh approaches to challenges by fostering an environment that supports and stimulates innovation. The teams, other cross-functional teams, and the company may find this useful. In the end, it will contribute to the organization's increased effectiveness and success.

Set an example for others

Strong leadership makes it simple for people to follow in your footsteps. It's not simply that you're in charge; it's also a result of your actions, abilities, and disposition. When you work well, you inspire your team to work well as well. Your words rarely have the same impact as your actions.

Setting a good example for your team will inspire them to aim for the same objectives since they will be able to see what outstanding technical accomplishments look like.

Enhanced Retention of Employees

A cohesive team that aspires to success and longevity will be formed by a strong technical leader. This will result in lower employee turnover and better employee retention. Employee retention is positively correlated with their perception of the company's support. They will experience a sense of belonging and empowerment within the organization.

Take on New Challenges

There is variation in every day. There are always highs and lows to it. Every step of the way, we must overcome obstacles and problems in life. In our daily lives as technical leaders, we must overcome these obstacles and challenges. We should anticipate obstacles to both people and technology.

Encourage mentorship

Most people view technical leaders as visionaries who can motivate every member of the team. You'll be able to help the group achieve its goals by setting new benchmarks for them to meet.

Strong technical leaders may make sure that the team generates higher-quality work by offering technical direction and coaching. Effective technical leaders can improve the productivity of their teams. They can help with technical decision-making, impart efficient problem-solving techniques, and guarantee that everyone agrees. As a result, the team as a whole produces more.

Making Decisions That Work

You should be a strong problem-solver as a technical leader. Any technological problems should be easy for you to troubleshoot and detect promptly. You won't have to spend as much time looking up answers or comparing options because you already know so much about the technical parts of the job. This will provide a quicker project pace and guarantee its timely completion. This will make it possible for you to promptly address any issues and guarantee that the team keeps up its productive work. When it comes to technical matters, you ought to be able to decide with certainty rather rapidly.

Encourage Innovation

As a good technical leader, you can assist teams in coming up with fresh approaches to challenges by fostering an environment that supports and stimulates innovation. The teams, other cross-functional teams, and the company may find this useful. In the end, it will contribute to the organization's increased effectiveness and success.

Barriers to Technical Leadership

Being a technical leader has its challenges, much like many other fields. It sounds more difficult than we could have imagined. Nothing worthwhile ever comes easily, is it? Although there may be some rough patches ahead, if we adhere to the previously mentioned portions, we can conquer the difficulties

below.
- ✓ Taking Charge Without Authority
- ✓ Managing Teams That Are Remote
- ✓ Task prioritization
- ✓ Settling disputes
- ✓ Juggling the demands of the organization and the team
- ✓ Adjusting to evolving technological landscapes
- ✓ Conveying technological ideas to non-technical people
- ✓ Establishing and preserving connections

Final Thought

In conclusion, a mix of essential qualities and abilities is needed to be a successful technical leader. Successful leadership is built on good communication, and staying current with industry trends and innovations requires ongoing learning. Making decisions requires the ability to navigate complexity and uncertainty, and setting a positive example for the team is vital to maintaining that attitude. Last but not least, mentoring is essential for assisting and motivating younger team members to advance and succeed. Technical leaders may successfully lead their teams, foster innovation, and succeed in the fast-paced, technologically-driven business world of today by exhibiting these qualities and abilities. Essential components of the art of technical leadership include adopting a growth attitude, remaining knowledgeable, communicating clearly, making wise judgments, fostering a good environment, and coaching team members. Technical leaders may motivate their people, effect positive change, and succeed in their positions by consistently improving these abilities.